ESSAYS IN INTERNATIONAL FINANCE
No. 181, March 1991

ON THE INTERNATIONAL USE OF CURRENCIES: THE CASE OF THE DEUTSCHE MARK

GEORGE S. TAVLAS

INTERNATIONAL FINANCE SECTION
DEPARTMENT OF ECONOMICS
PRINCETON UNIVERSITY
PRINCETON, NEW JERSEY

Library of Congress Cataloging-in-Publication Data

Tavlas, George S.
On the international use of currencies : the case of the deutsche mark / George S. Tavlas.
p. cm.—(Essays in international finance. ISSN 0071-142X ; no. 181)
Includes bibliographical references.
ISBN 0-88165-088-9 (pbk.) : $6.50
1. Money—Germany. 2. Foreign exchange problem—Germany. 3. International finance. 4. Economic history—1971- 5. Economic forecasting. I. Title. II. Series.
HG136.P7 no. 181
[HG999.5]
332'.042 s—dc20
[332.4'56'0943] 90-10869
CIP

Printed in the United States of America by Princeton University Press at Princeton, New Jersey

International Standard Serial Number: 0071-142X
International Standard Book Number: 0-88165-088-9
Library of Congress Catalog Card Number: 90-10869

CONTENTS

1 INTRODUCTION 1

2 THE CHOICE OF AN INTERNATIONAL CURRENCY: THEORETICAL CONSIDERATIONS 2

Overview 2
General Considerations 3
Vehicle Currencies 5
Some Applications: Hysteresis and the Current Account 9
Benefits and Costs of an International Currency 12

3 DETERMINANTS OF INTERNATIONAL CURRENCY USE: IMPLICATIONS FOR THE DEUTSCHE MARK 13

Inflation and the Credibility of Monetary Policy 13
Changes in Financial Markets 16
Changes in Foreign Trade 20

4 RECENT TRENDS 24

Currency-Invoicing Patterns 24
The Deutsche Mark as a Medium of Exchange 26
The Deutsche Mark as an Investment Currency 28

5 CONCLUSIONS 34

APPENDIX: Measures for Controlling Capital Inflows into Germany, 1970-89 36

REFERENCES 38

LIST OF TABLES

1 Inflation and Inflation Variability 14
2 Exchange-Rate Volatility 16
3 Exports and Imports as Shares of GDP, 1970-89 18
4 Export-Market Shares 21
5 Trade Shares by Major Partner Group 22
6 Shares of Exports by Product Category 23
7 Currency Invoicing of German Foreign Trade 25
8 Currency Denominations of World Exports 26
9 Currency Composition of Turnover in Major Foreign-Exchange Markets 27
10 Intervention in the EMS in Deutsche Marks 28
11 Currency Distribution of Foreign-Exchange Intervention 29
12 Foreign Deutsche-Mark Claims 30
13 Relative Currency Shares of External Assets 32
14 Currency Shares of Official Foreign-Exchange Holdings, 1980-89 33

ON THE INTERNATIONAL USE OF CURRENCIES: THE CASE OF THE DEUTSCHE MARK

1 Introduction

Since the move to a regime of managed floating exchange rates in 1973, the international monetary order has progressed gradually toward a multicurrency system. To be sure, the system continues to be dominated by the U.S. dollar, but other currencies—particularly the deutsche mark, yen, and Swiss franc—are being employed internationally with increasing regularity.

Despite the emergence of a multicurrency system, comprehensive and systematic discussions of factors underlying the international use of a currency and of recent trends toward internationalization have not been common. Most recent inquiry has focused on individual aspects of international currency use. Work on the deutsche mark, for example, has consisted of a series of informative studies dealing with the mark as an international investment currency (Deutsche Bundesbank, 1979, 1984, 1987); an article on the internationalization of German banking and finance (Neumann, 1986); a study on the role of the mark as a reserve asset (Rieke, 1982); and a study of the invoicing practices of German firms engaged in foreign trade (Scharrer, 1980). These discussions have been primarily descriptive; they have not provided systematic theoretical analyses or dealt with the interrelationships underlying the various uses of an international currency.

This essay attempts to fill the gap in the literature regarding the role of the deutsche mark as an international currency. It analyzes both theoretical aspects of external currency use and recent developments relating to the internationalization of the mark. The discussion is divided into four sections following this introduction. Section 2 deals with the conditions underlying the emergence of an international currency; theoretical considerations suggest that several important

I have benefited from helpful comments and suggestions by Joseph Aschheim, Martin Bailey, David Blond, Peter Clark, Warren Coats, Max Corden, Samir Fawzi, Insu Kim, Gerhard Laske, Thomas Mayer, Manfred Neumann, Yuzuru Ozeki, Ulrich Thiessen, Michael Ulan, David Williams, Manfred Willms, and an anonymous referee.

factors contribute to a currency's international use. Section 3 discusses these contributory factors as they relate to the deutsche mark and identifies trends in several of them that presage an expanding role for the mark. Section 4 describes recent developments that illustrate the growing international role of the deutsche mark during the 1980s. Section 5 provides concluding comments.

2 The Choice of an International Currency: Theoretical Considerations

Overview

The theory of international currency seeks to identify the factors that underlie the use of national monies as domestic financial instruments by nonresidents and as offshore financial instruments by both nonresidents and residents (for recent discussions of these factors, see Krugman, 1980, 1984; Kenen, 1983, 1988, chap. 5; Chrystal, 1984; Black, 1989; Frankel, 1989; Klump, 1989). In contrast to conventional definitions of domestic money, which typically focus on the short-term financial liabilities of the banking system and monetary authorities, the definition of international currency encompasses a broad spectrum of financial instruments. In addition, the theory of international currency attempts to explain the behavior of both private and official economic agents.

An international currency fulfills three basic functions in the international monetary system. It serves as a medium of exchange, a unit of account, and a store of value. As a *medium of exchange*, it is used by private agents both in direct exchange and as a vehicle of indirect exchange between two other currencies in foreign trade and international capital transactions. It is also used by official agents as a vehicle for intervention and for balance-of-payments financing. As a *unit of account*, it is used to invoice merchandise trade, to denominate financial transactions, and, by official agents, to define exchange-rate parities. As a *store of value*, it is used by private agents when choosing financial assets, such as bonds held by nonresidents. Similarly, official agents may hold an international currency and financial assets denominated in it as reserve assets.

What factors contribute to the use of a national money as an international currency? Why was the pound sterling the dominant international currency for so long, and why was its position subsequently supplanted by the U.S. dollar? Before addressing these issues, two observations are in order: (1) There is no comprehensive and rigorous theory that can accurately predict whether a national currency will become an international currency or whether the dominant international currency will soon be replaced by another. Theoretical discussion of international currency use is made difficult by the fact that, unlike the domestic choice of a currency, which is made by government fiat, the choice of currencies to be used for international transactions is predominantly "the result of 'invisible hand' processes ratified more than guided by international agreements" (Krugman, 1984, p. 261). Thus, the analysis of international currency use must account for the decisions of several distinct groups of economic agents whose reasons for using a specific currency can be quite diverse. Expectations that a particular currency will depreciate in value, for example, might prompt private agents to sell assets denominated in it. At the same time, however, central banks might enlarge their reserve holdings of that currency in a coordinated effort to support its value. (2) Theoretical investigations of international currency use are also complicated by geopolitical factors. Specifically, movements into or out of a currency for safe-haven considerations are not easily amenable to formal economic analysis.

For these reasons, the point of departure for the following discussion is, first, to set forth two sets of conditions that are generally shared by national monies used as international currencies—the coexistence of these conditions appears to be necessary for a currency to be used internationally—and, next, to derive a more specific set of supplementary conditions by investigating the determinants of the use of currencies as vehicles. These supplementary conditions reinforce the choice of a currency for international use, effectively determining the relative roles of various currencies.

The approach adopted in this essay differs from that taken in much of the previous analytic work by explaining international currency use as the outcome of dynamic processes dependent upon several necessary and reinforcing factors. Previous studies, by contrast, have often adopted a taxonomic approach (see, e.g., Fratianni, 1982), describing international currency use by function (as a medium of exchange, for example) and by agent (private or official), enumerating separately the factors that influence each subcategory but providing little insight into the interconnections, and thus the dynamics, involved.

General Considerations

Two sets of conditions must be satisfied before a currency can be used internationally. First, there must be confidence in the value of the currency and in the political stability of the issuing country. Specifically, relatively high and/or variable rates of inflation add to the costs of using a currency internationally by generating nominal-exchange-rate depreciation and variability. These factors increase the costs of acquiring information and making efficient calculations about the prices bid and offered for tradeable goods and capital assets. They thus undermine a currency's use as an international medium of exchange, unit of account, and store of value.[1] Furthermore, inflation increases the costs of holding a currency by eroding its purchasing power and thus debasing the currency as an international store of value and even as a medium of exchange, for international transactions often entail a lapse of time between the initiation and completion of a transaction.[2]

In the competitive environment that characterizes the choice among international currencies, economic agents understandably prefer currencies with relatively low inflation costs. As Kenen has observed, one of the key factors underlying the emergence of the U.S. dollar as the dominant international currency has been its "strength ... in terms of other currencies, backed by comparative price stability in the United States" (Kenen, 1988, p. 64). A protracted record of relatively low inflation and of low variability depends importantly on stable and consistent government policies. A history of current-account deficits in excess of normal private-capital inflows (those that occur in the absence of undue restrictions on trade or special incentives to incoming or outgoing capital) can lead to frequent exchange-rate depreciation, eroding confidence in the currency.

Second, a country should possess financial markets that are substantially free of controls; broad, in that they contain a large assortment of financial instruments; and deep, in that they have well-developed secondary markets. It should also possess financial institutions that are sophisticated and competitive in offshore financial centers.

The presence of financial-market controls increases the costs of transacting in a currency. For example, restrictions on the convertibility of a currency result in higher transfer costs (e.g., a greater likelihood of

[1] A number of recent studies have examined the costs of exchange-rate variability on the allocation of resources. For overviews of the literature, see Bailey and Tavlas (1988, 1991) and Williamson (1985).

[2] Surprisingly, much of the theoretical literature completely overlooks the role played by inflation in contributing to international currency use. Thus, Krugman (1980, 1984), one of the few writers who has attempted to provide systematic theoretical discussions of international currency use, omits all mention of the roles of relative inflation rates and credible government policies.

illiquidity), thereby impeding its use as an international currency. A country that is free of controls, however, and also possesses broad and deep financial markets is in a position to serve as an international banking center. Specifically, it can be expected to provide a high degree of efficiency in international liquidity transformation by accepting short-term, liquid liabilities denominated in its own currency while making long-term, less liquid loans abroad.

The view that a country with broad and deep financial markets has a comparative advantage in serving as an international banking center draws attention to the solvency risks incurred by a key-currency country when it functions as an international bank (Klump, 1989, pp. 387-392). The current-account and net-debtor positions of a country are important to the extent that they can affect confidence in a currency by increasing solvency risks and jeopardizing the functioning of a financial market as an international banking center.

In general, just as relatively low levels of inflation and inflation variability contribute to the international *demand* for a currency, well-developed financial markets are required to *supply* assets appropriate for international use (and to strengthen the demand for additional assets as well). Thus, the large financial markets of New York and London contribute to the use of the U.S. dollar and pound sterling, respectively, as international currencies.[3] By contrast, the Tokyo financial market, which was until recently rather tightly regulated, has inhibited the use of the yen as an international currency. Similarly, restrictions aimed at discouraging the use of the deutsche mark as a reserve currency restrained the international use of the mark for many years.

Vehicle Currencies

Private agents use a vehicle currency to denominate and execute foreign-trade and capital transactions that do not involve direct dealings with the issuing country. A currency is used as a vehicle when the transactions costs, including costs of information, search, uncertainty, and enforce-

[3] As Williams observed regarding sterling's earlier dominance as an international currency: "It was the international banking system centered in London which provided the heart of the operation of the sterling system of the pre-1914 decades" (1968, p. 270). Correspondingly, as Kenen has noted with respect to the emergence of the U.S. dollar as the key international currency after World War II, "U.S. financial markets were not fenced off by capital controls, so foreigners could lend and borrow freely. Therefore the dollar was an attractive reserve asset for official institutions and a convenient store of value for other foreign asset holders" (1988, pp. 63-64).

ment, are lower through the vehicle than through other, nonvehicle, currencies. Moreover, once a currency emerges as a vehicle, economies of scale enter into play, further decreasing transactions costs and enhancing the currency's position as a vehicle. For example, the more a currency is used, the greater the familiarity with it and the lower the costs of information and uncertainty—the greater, also, will be the probability of finding a matching transaction and thus the lower the search costs. Hence, vehicles develop as part of the innovation process in financial markets. As Levich has noted, "a variety of powerful financial instruments exist because they can establish equivalent financial positions at lower costs than any other set of transactions" (Levich, 1987, p. 107).

The uses of a currency as a vehicle for both invoicing and medium-of-exchange purposes are not unrelated. In fact, the numeraire function determines to a significant extent the currency used as a means of payment. Once a contract is denominated in, say, the exporter's currency, the medium-of-exchange function emerges as a by-product. Measures can be taken to hedge foreign-exchange risk, but, at the time of settlement, payment is typically made and accepted in the same currency. The relationship is not a tight one, however, and need not hold, even within a domestic economy. During the German hyperinflation of the 1920s, for example, gold marks served as the unit of account, but payment was often made in U.S. dollars.

What specific set of influences contributes to the determination of invoicing behavior? A number of empirical studies investigating invoicing practices between exporters and importers have found typical patterns of behavior (see, e.g., Grassman, 1973; Page, 1977, 1981; Carse et al., 1980; Magee and Rao, 1980; Scharrer, 1980; and Bilson, 1983, 1987). Analyzing these patterns can shed light on the objectives that are important in decisionmaking by firms and, more specifically, on the firms' attitudes toward foreign-exchange risk. The observed patterns are that:

(1) Trade between developed countries in manufactured products is likely to be invoiced in the exporter's currency. Note, however, that this pattern is influenced by the presence of the general conditions discussed above. Thus, throughout the 1970s, a relatively small proportion of Japanese exports, particularly to the United States, was denominated in yen. This was attributable in part to "the reluctance of the Japanese government to allow the yen to become an international trading currency" (Page, 1981, p. 64).

(2) Currency hedging by importers in forward markets is rather uncommon.

(3) Invoicing in the exporter's currency is most frequent for differen-

tiated manufactured products with long contractual lags.

(4) Trade between developed and less-developed countries tends to be denominated in the currency of the developed country, although the U.S. dollar is also used frequently. This pattern is known as Grassman's Law.

(5) Trade in primary products is usually denominated in U.S. dollars and, to a lesser extent, in sterling.

How can these apparently diverse patterns of behavior be synthesized? To accommodate them within a single framework, it is important to note that the income or costs of an exporter or importer who uses a foreign currency and does not hedge will be affected immediately in terms of his domestic currency whenever the exchange rate changes. Correspondingly, there will be no effect on his income from contracts that are already fixed if he uses his own currency. As Page has observed, "traders tend to prefer their own currency because they are adverse to risk, and particularly unwilling to engage in managing foreign exchange exposures" (Page, 1981, p. 70).

If importers are risk averse, why do they often refrain from currency hedging when contracts are denominated in the exporter's currency? Bilson (1983) points out that forward markets are typically thinner than spot markets and thus usually entail larger bid-ask spreads. In addition, invoicing in the exporter's currency provides an important hedge for the importer (McKinnon, 1979; Bilson, 1983). Specifically, both the importer and exporter consider the variance of their respective profits in making the invoicing decision. The covariance between revenue and costs, however, is likely to be higher for the importer than for the exporter, particularly for an exporter of manufactured products, the costs for which are determined early in the production process. Consequently, it is harder for exporters to cut their factor costs in response to a depreciation of their currencies. They have to absorb unfavorable exchange-rate movements in lower profit margins. Exporters, therefore, have an incentive to invoice in their own currencies (McKinnon, 1979, pp. 68-69).

Exporters can hedge, of course, but the use of the forward market increases their costs. The longer the contractual lag, the higher the risk that an exchange-rate change will ensue and the higher also the exporters' incentive to denominate in their own currency. In addition, as McKinnon and Page have noted, producers of differentiated (if only in brand name) manufactured products often possess a degree of monopolistic power, and they may exploit it to shift risk to their customers (McKinnon, 1979, p. 74; Page, 1981, p. 62). Onc would therefore expect the share of the exporter's currency to vary with the monopoly power of the exporter and thus to rise with the degree of product differentiation.

In contrast, the market situation of the importer provides a natural hedge against some of the currency risk assumed by denominating contracts in the exporter's currency. The importer can often pass through an exchange-rate depreciation by charging a higher price for the product in the domestic market. This course of action is most practical in the absence of a large domestic import-competing industry. Hence, small countries that are open, in the sense that they are characterized by substantial and rapid "pass through," are more likely to use the currency of an exporter of differentiated manufactured products.

To the extent that the importer bears some risk by contracting in the exporter's currency, he gains expertise in dealing with that risk. As Krugman has stated: "the importer ... has to deal with exchange markets as a matter of course.... In small countries, everyone is obliged to be sophisticated about foreign exchange" (Krugman, 1984, p. 271). Indeed, such sophistication can be turned to the importer's advantage. The fact that importers gain knowledge through trade helps them "anticipate future exchange rate movements better than the average participant in the foreign exchange market. If so, the profitability of this knowledge could offset the risk of exchange rate volatility," (Bailey and Tavlas, 1988, p. 431).

The likelihood, therefore, that the exporter's currency will be used as the invoicing vehicle is greater the larger that country's share of world exports, the more its exports are comprised of differentiated manufactured products, and the larger its share of products that are imported by developing countries. Note, however, that these generalizations need not apply symmetrically. The United States, for example, exports proportionately fewer manufactured goods than does Germany, but a high proportion of its total exports is denominated in dollars, partly because prices for its relatively large share of commodity exports are typically denominated in dollars. Similarly, a higher proportion of German exports is invoiced in deutsche marks than would be the case if Germany exported relatively more primary products, which are, again, generally denominated in U.S. dollars. Note also that a growing percentage of German exports is directed toward other, developed, countries of the European Community (EC), but these countries have increased the proportion of their imports invoiced in deutsche marks. Consequently, the redirection of German exports from developing countries to EC countries has not necessarily reduced the share of German exports invoiced in deutsche marks.

The wider the use of a currency as a vehicle, the more familiar it becomes and the smaller the associated information and search costs. This observation is particularly important in explaining why primary products and financial instruments are usually denominated in vehicle currencies.

Primary products and financial assets share several common attributes. They are characterized by low levels of product differentiation and they are traded in competitive markets, in which use of a widely known currency as a numeraire minimizes costs of information and calculation. Using a vehicle currency for trade in these competitive markets facilitates the efficient communication of competitors' prices and may therefore be preferred by both exporters and importers (Magee and Rao, 1980). With differentiated products, by contrast, the markets are less competitive, and information about competitors' prices is less important.

To summarize briefly, two sets of conditions are necessary for the international use of a nation's currency, confidence in the value of the currency, and the presence of well-developed financial markets that are free of controls. These conditions help to explain the emergence of the U.S. dollar as an international currency; correspondingly, the absence of a well-developed, control-free financial market helps to explain the relatively insignificant use of the yen internationally during the 1970s. These conditions do not by themselves, however, fully explain why a particular currency emerges as the dominant international currency. Dominance appears to be directly related to the issuing country's share of world exports, to the proportion of its exports comprising specialized manufactured products, and to the extent of its trade with developing countries. The combination of these factors fosters vehicle use and generates familiarity and confidence that encourage the use of the currency in primary-product and financial-asset markets, further lowering transactions costs and reinforcing international currency use.

Some Applications: Hysteresis and the Current Account

The preceding analysis can help explain behavioral patterns that have been examined in a rather cursory fashion in much of the literature. For example, the dynamics of international currency use are often ascribed to such concepts as "hysteresis," with little attention given to the process underlying the notion. Thus, sterling's continued use as an international currency, despite the decline in the United Kingdom's share of world trade, has been attributed to "inertia" in the system (Krugman, 1984, pp. 268-269; also Frankel, 1989, p. 1, and Glynn, 1989, p. 163). In a world of efficient markets, however, "inertia" is hard to explain. In fact, sterling continues to be an international currency because London is a sophisticated financial center and because the United Kingdom is still among the largest suppliers of merchandise exports to the world. As Williams noted: "The long-term growth of 'sterling balances' after 1900 was mainly a reflection of the growth of commercial banking in the world, and the convenience of settling international debts in cash and holding surplus funds for this purpose in a money market [i.e., London] which offered a plethora of investment opportunities" (Williams, 1968, pp. 286-287). These considerations still apply.

Correspondingly, several factors combined to undermine the role of sterling as the dominant international currency. These include (1) a number of sharp fluctuations in sterling's external value beginning in the late 1940s. These were induced in part by high inflation in the United Kingdom relative to that of its trading partners, which made it more difficult for London to attract short-term capital from the nonsterling world; (2) the continuation of exchange and other controls, which limited London's efficiency in international liquidity transformation after World War II, in contrast to the relative openness of the U.S. financial market; and (3) the decline in the share of world trade accounted for by sterling-area countries after World War II (McKinnon, 1979, p. 169, and Williams, 1968, pp. 293-294).

The foregoing analysis helps also to explain some inconsistencies in previous discussions of international currency use. Some writers have argued that a nation's position as a net-capital exporter is an important determinant of international currency use (see, e.g., Frankel, 1989); large and persistent current-account surpluses accompanied by capital outflows supposedly encourage the internationalization of a currency. This surplus/outflow pattern has been cited to explain the growing uses of the yen and the deutsche mark as international currencies. The explanation is inconsistent, however, with the fact that the United States has recorded large current-account deficits for a number of years. The dollar continues to be the dominant international currency, although its share of international use has declined. By the same token, the Australian dollar emerged as an international currency during the 1980s, in that it was (and is) one of the most actively traded currencies in foreign-exchange markets. At the same time, however, Australia recorded annual current-account deficits equivalent to about 5 percent of GDP. Underpinning the international use of the Australian dollar has been the complete deregulation of the Australian financial system, which was tightly controlled until 1980.[4] The important criterion in this regard is not whether a country records net-capital

[4] See Swamy and Tavlas (1989, 1991). By way of comparison, the Australian dollar exhibited virtually no signs of international use in the 1970s, although Australian current-account deficits were smaller, averaging about 2 percent of GDP. In 1989, the Australian dollar was the seventh most actively traded currency in New York (Federal Reserve Bank of New York, 1989).

inflows or outflows, but whether these affect confidence in a currency, which, in turn, affects the solvency of the country and its ability to function as an international banking center. For this purpose, the investments for which capital inflows are used should provide rates of return higher than the cost of borrowing. As Frenkel and Goldstein observe, this further assumes that the order of magnitude of capital inflows is "compatible over the long run with a reasonable build-up of debt" (Frenkel and Goldstein, 1986, p. 645).

A common element underlying the external positions of Germany, Japan, and the United States is not their respective current-account positions, which may or may not be running surpluses or deficits; it is that they are the three largest suppliers of merchandise exports to the world. Furthermore, sizeable shares of their exports go to developing countries and are comprised of differentiated manufactured products; this point is discussed in more detail below, in connection with the role of the deutsche mark.

Given the necessary conditions for international currency use, a current-account surplus over a protracted period can serve as a promotional mechanism for the international use of a nation's currency. For example, in recent years, Germany and Japan have been running current-account surpluses; in effect, they have been selling goods, buying bonds and equities, and making direct investments. The promotional mechanics underlying this process are that (1) the net export of capital in, say, deutsche marks can induce foreigners to acquire deutsche-mark balances in order to service mark-denominated obligations and (2) because the net transfer of liquidity from the surplus entity (e.g., Germany) to deficit entities is accompanied by the net transfer of goods and/or services in the same direction, the international use of the currency issued by the nation will be enhanced as foreigners demand claims in the currency of the exporter so they can pay for imports from the surplus nation (Tavlas and Ozeki, 1991, p. 20).

If, however, Japan and Germany continue to run current-account surpluses, will there be sufficient supplies of deutsche marks and yen (and of assets denominated in them) to use as international currencies? On the surface, this question seems to evoke concerns raised by the so-called dollar shortage after World War II, when persistent U.S. current-account surpluses were associated with an excess demand for the dollar at prevailing exchange rates. In fact, however, the two cases are quite distinct. In the early postwar period, the dollar shortage was dealt with by a variety of devices, including measures by the United States to stimulate imports, restrictions by most countries on foreign-exchange transactions, and occasional devaluations. By contrast, in today's world of highly mobile capital and flexible exchange rates, the possibility of a currency shortage is less pertinent. For one thing, capital-account transactions dwarf current-account flows. For another, the prices of currencies move to equate demands and supplies. If people want a particular currency and assets denominated in it, they can obtain them provided they are willing to pay the market price. In addition, a country can run current-account surpluses and yet provide liquidity to the rest of the world if it is also a net exporter of short-term capital.

Benefits and Costs of an International Currency

International currency use provides two major benefits to the issuing country. First, the country derives seigniorage because the foreign claims built up on it are denominated in its own currency. And, because the nominal interest rate on debt is comprised of a real component and an expected-inflation component, countries with international currencies can inflate away an arbitrarily large portion of the real purchasing power represented by their nominal debt by policies that raise the inflation rate above its expected level. Countries for which the external debt is denominated in foreign currencies must earn foreign currency to service those claims. As Cohen has noted: "The [key-currency] country obtains a kind of free command over real resources which can be used to enlarge its purchase of foreign goods, services and assets" (Cohen, 1971, p. 35). In effect, foreigners extend credit to the issuing (key-currency) country, but at the prevailing interest rate.

Second, as the international use of a currency expands, loans, investments, and purchases of goods and services will increasingly be executed through the financial institutions of the issuing country. Thus, the earnings of its financial sector are likely to increase (Cohen, 1971, p. 37). In addition, the issuing country's exporters and importers, as well as borrowers and lenders, gain a comparative advantage over, and have less risk than, their foreign competitors and customers, for they are dealing in a currency in which their costs are denominated and with which they have more familiarity than the foreigners. To the extent that foreigners also become familiar with the currency, information costs will decrease for them as well, thereby increasing the currency's use as a vehicle.

The main cost typically ascribed to the international use of a currency is the diminished scope for controlling its supply domestically. Throughout the 1970s and into the 1980s, the German and Japanese monetary authorities imposed controls on capital flows in order to increase their influence over the money supply. This need not be necessary, however, if the monetary authorities do not intervene in the foreign-exchange market but instead allow fluctuations in the demand for the currency to affect the exchange rate.

An additional cost of international currency use involves an offset to the seigniorage used to service foreign claims. The temptation to exploit seigniorage can lead to higher inflation in the key-currency country and can thus eventually undermine one of the essential prerequisites for using its currency internationally.

3 Determinants of International Currency Use: Implications for the Deutsche Mark

The preceding section has identified a number of factors contributing to the international use of a currency. To understand the implications of these factors with respect to the deutsche mark, the following discussion assesses Germany's historical record on inflation, the institutional characteristics of German financial markets, and relevant features of Germany's foreign trade. Because the influence of these factors depends upon comparisons with other major countries, the discussion considers, to the extent feasible, the position of Germany relative to other major industrial countries.

Inflation and the Credibility of Monetary Policy

Since 1975, monetary policy in Germany has followed a medium-term orientation "with a view to keeping the value of money stable" (Deutsche Bundesbank, 1988, p. 22). To this end, the Bundesbank adopted monetary targeting in 1975. Underlying its medium-term approach to formulating monetary policy is the view that monetary growth is an important determinant of nominal income growth and of the balance of payments in the short term, but that its primary impact over the medium term is on inflation and the nominal exchange rate. Consequently, a stable, medium-term orientation for monetary policy provides credibility, lowers inflationary expectations, reduces uncertainty, and contributes to a climate conducive to capital formation.

A medium-term, anti-inflationary orientation for monetary policy was also adopted during the 1970s by the United States, the United Kingdom, Japan, France, Switzerland, and Italy. The outcomes of these policies in terms of the inflation objective are reported in Table 1, which presents the average annual inflation rates for these countries and Germany from 1970 to 1989 and for four subperiods. Germany experienced the lowest average inflation rate among the seven, followed by Switzerland and

Japan. Table 1 also reports the standard deviations of national inflation rates as a measure of inflation variability. These figures tell a similar story. Over the 1970-89 period, Germany experienced the lowest inflation variability, followed by Switzerland and the United States.

These data indicate that, relative to other major industrial countries, Germany's monetary policy has successfully maintained a stable internal value for the deutsche mark. This has, according to the Bundesbank, procured credibility for Germany's monetary policy to the extent that "within the European Monetary System, [the deutsche mark] performs the function of a key currency, acting as a 'stability anchor' for the other pertinent currencies" (Deutsche Bundesbank, 1988, p. 14). Similarly, Fischer describes the European Monetary System (EMS) as "an arrangement for France and Italy to purchase a commitment to low inflation by accepting German monetary policy" (Fischer, 1987, pp. 22-23). Even in

TABLE 1

INFLATION AND INFLATION VARIABILITY

(*percent*)

Period	Germany	United States	United Kingdom	Japan	France	Switzerland	Italy
			Average Inflation Rate				
1970-74	5.6	6.1	9.6	10.7	7.7	7.1	9.1
1975-79	4.2	8.1	15.7	7.5	10.2	2.9	15.9
1980-84	4.5	7.5	9.6	3.9	11.2	4.4	16.6
1985-89	1.3	3.6	5.3	1.2	3.6	2.1	6.2
1970-89	3.9	6.3	10.0	5.8	8.1	4.1	11.9
			Inflation Variability [a]				
1970-74	1.3	2.8	3.6	6.8	3.2	2.3	5.8
1975-79	1.2	2.2	5.8	3.3	1.2	2.4	3.5
1980-84	1.5	3.9	5.2	2.2	2.4	1.6	3.8
1985-89	1.2	1.1	1.7	1.0	1.3	1.1	1.7
1970-89 [b]	2.1	3.2	5.7	5.4	3.6	2.7	5.9

SOURCE: International Monetary Fund, *International Financial Statistics*, various issues, 1981-90.

[a] Based on consumer price indices; variability measured by standard deviation using quarterly data for indicated periods.

[b] The average of the sum of the standard deviations does not necessarily equal the average standard deviation for the entire period.

countries that consider EMS membership, the main advantages of membership are associated with Germany's reputation. Thus, according to the *Financial Times*: "In place of money supply targetry, long since discredited, we would have that unflinching guardian of monetary rectitude, the Bundesbank, standing as guarantor against Britain's endemic propensity to generate double-figure rates of inflation" (*Financial Times*, September 28, 1987).

In fact, the willingness of other EC countries to emulate Germany illustrates precisely the argument made earlier regarding the factors that influence international currency use, that is, that a low and stable inflation rate supports internationalization. Other members of the Exchange Rate Mechanism (ERM) of the EMS have effectively elected to use the deutsche mark as their numeraire by pegging their currencies to it. As Kenen has observed: "By pegging their currencies to the German mark, they [the members of the ERM] linked their monetary policies to those of the Bundesbank and thus borrowed some of its credibility as an implacable foe of inflation" (Kenen, 1988, pp. 18-19). A number of writers have even characterized the ERM as a "deutsche mark zone" (see, e.g., Dornbusch, 1986).

Germany also derives benefits from participation in the Exchange Rate Mechanism of the EMS. These include some retention of domestic monetary independence (Melitz, 1988, p. 68) and decreased volatility of the nominal exchange rate against the other EMS currencies (Ungerer et al., 1986; Deutsche Bundesbank, 1988, pp. 13-14; Giavazzi and Giovannini, 1989, pp. 197-198).[5] Table 2 examines the volatility of nominal effective rates for the same countries covered in Table 1. Over the 1975-89 period, the deutsche mark's volatility was the lowest among the seven currencies. In real effective terms, moreover, the mark appreciated slightly (9 percent) during that period and displayed much less volatility than did real exchange rates for the U.S. dollar, pound sterling, and yen.

One can conclude from the above that (1) German monetary policy, formulated in a medium-term context with the aim of controlling inflation, has been relatively successful in achieving that objective, which has enhanced the Bundesbank's credibility; (2) the Bundesbank's success in

[5] Some writers have suggested that the ERM has resulted in a lower real exchange rate for the deutsche mark than would otherwise have been the case. According to their hypothesis, the tendency within the ERM to maintain stable nominal exchange rates while inflation rates have not yet converged implies a trendwise real depreciation for the deutsche mark (Melitz, 1988). Empirical support has not been provided for this hypothesis, however.

TABLE 2

EXCHANGE-RATE VOLATILITY

(*percent*)

Period	Germany	United States	United Kingdom	Japan	France	Switzerland	Italy
1975-79	1.1	1.3	1.9	2.2	1.2	1.8	1.8
1980-84	1.0	2.0	1.8	2.2	1.1	1.6	0.7
1985-89	0.8	2.2	2.0	2.1	0.7	1.3	0.7
1975-89 [a]	1.0	2.0	1.9	2.2	1.1	1.6	1.2
			Average Real Effective Exchange Rate (*1975 = 100*)				
1989	109.0	91.9	134.2	122.0	81.8	98.7	103.7

SOURCE: International Monetary Fund, *International Financial Statistics*, various issues, 1981-90.

NOTE: Calculated as standard deviation of monthly percentage change in the nominal MERM rate.

[a] The average of the sum of the standard deviations does not necessarily equal the average standard deviation for the entire period.

maintaining a stable internal value for the deutsche mark has contributed substantially to its stable external value; (3) the formation of the EMS has also contributed to a more stable external value for the mark, and the credibility of the Bundesbank has increased the willingness of other countries to participate in the ERM and to use the deutsche mark as an anchor; and (4) Germany's economic policies, particularly with regard to price stability, have played a crucial role in increasing the international use of the deutsche mark.

Changes in Financial Markets

Between the late 1960s and early 1980s, the Bundesbank attempted to limit the international use of the deutsche mark. Underlying this approach, which emerged under the Bretton Woods regime of fixed exchange rates, was the view that substantial swings in capital flows could interfere with domestic stabilization. In 1972 and early 1973, for example, restrictive monetary measures aimed at lowering inflation were implemented. These measures induced capital inflows, and the Bundesbank was forced to intervene to support the U.S. dollar; to offset the effects of intervention on the money supply, the Bundesbank took more restrictive monetary measures, which led to more capital inflows, and so on.[6] To tighten its grip on domestic monetary conditions, the Bundesbank extended relatively firm control over the issue of deutsche-mark obligations in the external bond market and international money market (Neumann, 1986, p. 110). During the early 1970s, moreover, the Bundesbank imposed higher minimum-reserve ratios on deposits owed to nonresidents than on deposits owed to residents. Although the move to a flexible exchange rate in 1973 increased the Bundesbank's potential control over domestic monetary conditions, the gain in control for Germany may have been less than for other large developed countries, in view of the relative openness of Germany's economy (Table 3).[7]

German restrictions on capital movements were directed primarily at inflows, which were relatively free compared with conditions in many other countries; controls on capital outflows had been relaxed during the 1950s, with the emergence of current-account surpluses, steady increases in external reserves, and the settlement of German external debts (Deutsche Bundesbank, 1985, p. 16). The most important restriction placed on capital inflows involved a "gentlemen's agreement" between the Bundesbank and the German banks in 1968. This agreement pertained to the issuance of foreign deutsche-mark bonds, which had become increasingly popular in the late 1960s. Because Germany's capital market was still very narrow, however, large issues of these bonds at times "had an adverse effect on the [operation of] Germany's capital market" (Deutsche Bundesbank, 1985, p. 14). A move by the Bundesbank to tighten monetary conditions could, for example, be undermined to some degree by the availability of credit in the Euromarket.

The gentlemen's agreement stipulated that only German banks could lead syndicates to issue bonds denominated in deutsche marks and that the volume of issues would be subject to the approval of a central capital-market committee (Thomas, 1987). Underlying the agreement was the belief that German banks would be more apt to follow the advice of the Bundesbank than would foreign banks (Neumann, 1986, pp. 109-110). Foreign issuing houses and their German subsidiaries were allowed to

[6] The example is from Goldstein, who notes that, "in February and March of 1973 alone, the Deutsche Bundesbank purchased $8.5 billion—only to succumb to floating rates the next month" (1984, p. 21).

[7] According to the theory of optimum currency areas, exchange-rate fluctuations induce larger domestic price changes in more open economies, thereby complicating the task of domestic stabilization policies and contributing to a preference for a stable exchange rate. See, for example, Aschheim and Park (1976).

TABLE 3

EXPORTS AND IMPORTS AS SHARES OF GDP, 1970-89
(*percent*)

Period	Germany	United States	United Kingdom	Japan	France
1970-74	36.0	10.2	36.6	19.8	29.1
1975-79	42.0	14.7	44.4	21.5	35.2
1980-84	49.7	15.9	42.1	24.6	38.8
1985-89	49.6	15.3	43.6	18.0	36.9

SOURCE: International Monetary Fund, *International Financial Statistics*, various issues, 1981-90.

NOTE: Averages of sums of exports and imports as shares of GDP; calculated from data denominated in respective national currencies.

participate as co-managers in deutsche-mark Eurobond syndicates but were excluded from the more attractive role of co-lead management.

Another important restriction concerned the kinds of bond issues allowed; only the standard fixed-rate issue was permitted. Innovative financial instruments, such as floating-rate notes, zero-coupon bonds, and bonds linked to currency and interest-rate swaps, were strictly prohibited.

These and other restrictions weakened the competitive position of German banks vis-à-vis foreign banks and led to innovations aimed at avoiding the regulations. For example, the worldwide upsurge and increased variability of inflation rates during the 1970s rendered fixed-rate bonds less attractive than other, more flexible, instruments. Concurrently, technological improvements (e.g., in data processing) lowered transaction costs, making it easier for regulated institutions to circumvent restrictions by financial innovation. In this environment of rapid innovation, the Bundesbank discovered in 1983 that a foreign deutsche-mark bond issue had been used to arrange a currency swap. Currency swaps were fairly new at that time and had not yet been prohibited; the Bundesbank therefore stepped in formally and restricted their future use. The restrictions on lead management by foreign banks led to retaliation against German banks, which also worked to weaken their competitive position. Foreign banks were less likely to accept German banks as co-lead managers of other Eurocurrency bond issues (Neumann, 1986).

By the mid-1980s, the Bundesbank's position had changed substantially, and the bank acknowledged the difficulty of inhibiting the operation of market forces underlying the demand for assets denominated in deutsche marks. In its *Monthly Report* of July 1985, the Bundesbank stated: "In view of the international role of the deutsche mark, Germany cannot shut itself off from the trend which is now under way, since the deutsche mark must remain competitive against [other] international investment currencies" (Deutsche Bundesbank, 1985, p. 14). By the mid-1980s, moreover, German financial markets had developed markedly and were better insulated from external disturbances. Consequently, most restrictions on the issuance of foreign deutsche-mark bonds have been lifted. The major measures liberalizing capital imports are listed in the Appendix.

Although most restrictions on bond issues have been lifted—the main remaining one being that deutsche-mark issues must be made in Germany—German financial markets have lagged behind those in other large financial centers, most notably London and New York, in several respects (Storch, 1989). A turnover tax on all secondary-market dealings in bonds and equities has prevented the establishment of a market in short-term commercial paper and has encouraged the switching of secondary trading in deutsche-mark paper to financial centers outside Germany (Thomas, 1987).[8] This tax also discriminates in favor of public-sector bonds, which are exempt, and has thus contributed to a narrow bond market dominated by public-sector issues. Furthermore, the equity market is thin and trading is narrow; the issuance of shares is said to be relatively expensive for want of competition in underwriting activity; and private pension plans are less active in the German stock market than in some other countries, reflecting in part the comprehensive nature of the social security system. Finally, because futures trading has not been allowed in Germany, futures activity involving German firms has been directed to London and Paris (Storch, 1989, p. 9).

Measures have been taken to enhance Germany's competitiveness. It was announced in late 1989 that the turnover tax would be revoked in 1991, and futures trading has been allowed in Frankfurt since early 1990. Nevertheless, the fact that Germany has lagged behind other financial centers has restricted its relative efficiency in international liquidity transformation.

The 1970s and 1980s saw a sharp increase in the number of German banks operating in foreign countries and in foreign banks operating in Germany. The number of foreign subsidiaries and branches of German banks rose from only 8 in 1970 to 186 in 1988, and the number of

[8] Another factor that inhibited competitiveness for a time was a withholding tax on interest income, including income earned by foreigners who could not take advantage of exemptions under existing tax treaties. The withholding tax was announced in late 1987, took effect from January 1989, but was abolished as of July 1989.

branches of foreign banks operating in Germany rose from 25 in 1970 to 58 in 1988 (Deutsche Bundesbank, 1988).

Initially, the internationalization of German banks involved the establishment of consortium banks (joint ventures with foreign banks), which afforded the opportunity of going international with limited investment. Conflicts among member banks over the consortium's policies, however, led to increased use of foreign branches and subsidiaries as vehicles for internationalization.

Several other developments contributed to the internationalization of German banking. First, the expansion of German exports created a situation in which "the larger export companies and their foreign affiliates had a demand for a service and financial assistance which in principle could be more cheaply provided by their German bankers, [for] the latter had an information-cost advantage over foreign banks" (Neumann, 1986, p. 76). Second, the emergence of the Eurodollar market posed a competitive threat to the German banks and contributed to their expansion into foreign financial centers. Similarly, the lifting of restrictions on foreign branches operating in Germany, including the prohibitions on interest payments to foreign depositors and on sales of domestic money-market paper to nonresidents, was conducive to the increased presence of foreign banks in Germany (Neumann, 1986, pp. 75-81).

Changes in Foreign Trade

Data pertaining to trade patterns during the 1980s are reported in Tables 4, 5, and 6. Table 4 shows that export-market shares rose substantially for Germany and Japan and slightly for the United States, but remained the same for France and declined for the United Kingdom. Because a country's share in world exports has been found to be an important determinant of invoicing behavior, the potential of the deutsche mark as an invoicing vehicle appears to have been enhanced during the 1980s.

Another factor influencing invoicing practices is the extent of trade with developing countries. Table 4 reports two factors that would indicate a smaller use of the deutsche mark as an invoicing vehicle in the absence of Germany's growing share of total world trade. First, Germany's share of developing-country markets declined between 1980 and 1989, whereas Japan's share rose. Second, the United States remains the world's largest exporter to developing countries.

Table 5 reports data on the direction of trade for the same set of countries, expressed as shares of each country's total exports and imports. In all instances, both exports to and imports from developing countries declined. In 1988 and 1989, moreover, Germany's export and import

TABLE 4

EXPORT-MARKET SHARES

(percent)

Exporters and Markets	1980	1982	1984	1986	1988	1989
Germany						
World	9.9	9.8	9.3	11.7	11.7	11.4
Industrial countries	10.5	10.6	10.0	12.7	13.0	13.1
Developing countries	7.5	7.4	6.6	7.9	6.7	6.5
United States						
World	11.3	11.8	11.8	10.5	11.6	12.1
Industrial countries	9.2	9.6	10.0	9.0	9.7	10.3
Developing countries	15.7	15.7	15.2	15.3	16.7	16.8
United Kingdom						
World	5.7	5.4	5.1	5.2	5.2	5.1
Industrial countries	5.6	5.6	5.4	5.3	5.5	5.4
Developing countries	5.6	4.9	4.2	4.5	4.1	3.9
Japan						
World	6.7	7.7	9.2	10.2	9.5	9.2
Industrial countries	4.3	5.4	7.2	8.5	7.7	7.4
Developing countries	11.0	11.4	12.7	13.1	14.5	13.7
France						
World	6.0	5.4	5.3	6.0	6.1	6.0
Industrial counties	5.5	5.0	4.9	5.8	6.2	6.1
Developing countries	5.7	5.2	5.0	5.3	4.3	4.6

SOURCES: International Monetary Fund, *International Financial Statistics, Supplement on Trade Statistics*, 1990, and IMF staff calculations.

NOTE: Computed from data expressed in U.S. dollars.

trade with developing countries was lower, relative to its total trade, than that of any other country.

The final factor influencing invoicing behavior is the share of differentiated manufactured products in a country's total exports. Table 6 presents data on exports by product group for Germany, the United States, and Japan, with exports in each product group expressed as a share of the country's total exports. The product group that contains specialized manufactured goods with long production lags is machinery and transport equipment (SITC 7). Although that group's share of total German exports rose between 1980 and 1989, the United States and Japan also recorded substantial increases.

This survey has identified several developments that together imply a

TABLE 5

TRADE SHARES BY MAJOR PARTNER GROUP

(percent of country total)

Exporter and Partner Group	1980		1982		1984		1986		1988		1989	
	Exports	Imports	Exports	Imports	Exports	Imports	Exports	Imports	Exports	Imports	Exports	Imports
Germany												
Industrial countries	74.4	71.3	73.0	72.9	76.4	74.3	79.9	77.9	81.3	78.6	82.8	79.9
Developing countries	25.6	28.7	27.0	27.1	23.6	25.7	20.1	22.1	18.7	21.4	17.2	20.1
United States												
Industrial countries	56.8	49.2	55.2	56.4	59.9	59.8	63.2	64.6	62.1	61.3	63.2	60.0
Developing countries	43.2	50.8	44.8	43.6	40.1	40.2	36.8	35.4	37.9	38.7	36.8	40.0
United Kingdom												
Industrial countries	69.6	75.0	70.5	78.4	75.0	80.4	75.7	82.3	76.5	83.0	78.5	84.2
Developing countries	30.4	25.0	29.5	21.6	25.0	19.6	24.3	17.7	23.5	27.0	21.5	15.8
Japan												
Industrial countries	45.3	33.6	47.3	35.2	55.3	38.8	61.5	47.3	60.1	49.5	60.3	50.0
Developing countries	54.7	66.4	42.7	64.8	44.7	61.2	42.4	52.7	38.8	51.5	29.7	50.0
France												
Industrial countries	65.0	65.9	63.2	67.8	66.3	70.7	71.2	77.4	74.5	77.8	75.3	79.2
Developing countries	35.0	34.1	36.8	32.2	33.7	28.3	28.8	22.6	25.5	22.2	24.7	20.1

SOURCES: International Monetary Fund, *International Financial Statistics, Supplement on Trade Statistics*, 1990, and IMF staff calculations.

NOTE: Trade with IMF's industrial-country and developing-country groups expressed as shares of country's total exports and imports. Developing-country group includes IMF's "other countries" category.

TABLE 6

SHARES OF EXPORTS BY PRODUCT CATEGORY

(percent)

Product Group and Exporter	1980	1982	1984	1986	1988	1989
Food products						
Germany	7.0	7.0	7.0	7.0	6.0	6.0
United States	22.0	22.0	20.0	18.0	17.0	16.0
Japan	2.0	1.0	1.0	1.0	1.0	1.0
Materials and fuels						
Germany	8.0	6.0	6.0	5.0	5.0	5.0
United States	17.0	15.0	15.0	10.0	13.0	11.0
Japan	3.0	2.0	1.0	2.0	1.0	2.0
Chemicals						
Germany	5.0	13.0	15.0	14.0	13.0	12.0
United States	10.0	10.0	11.0	11.0	9.0	9.0
Japan	6.0	5.0	5.0	5.0	5.0	5.0
Intermediate manufactured goods						
Germany	23.0	18.0	19.0	18.0	17.0	17.0
United States	12.0	8.0	7.0	7.0	8.0	8.0
Japan	27.0	22.0	18.0	15.0	13.0	13.0
Machinery and transport equipment						
Germany	38.0	45.0	42.0	44.0	46.0	47.0
United States	32.0	38.0	40.0	41.0	45.0	44.0
Japan	52.0	61.0	65.0	68.0	71.0	71.0
Consumer goods						
Germany	10.0	11.0	12.0	12.0	13.0	13.0
United States	7.0	6.0	8.0	8.0	9.0	10.0
Japan	11.0	10.0	10.0	9.0	9.0	9.0

SOURCE: Date Resources, *World Trade Model Data Book*, 1990.

growing role for the deutsche mark as an international currency: (1) the importance of the deutsche mark within Europe has increased as a result of Germany's performance with respect to inflation, the credibility of German monetary policy, and the associated relative stability of the deutsche mark's external value; (2) a wider menu of financial instruments denominated in deutsche marks has been made available and there has been a lifting of the remaining controls on German capital imports; and

(3) Germany's share of merchandise exports to the world has increased. Some of these developments have also been characteristic of other countries. Japan and Switzerland, for example, have experienced relatively low inflation rates and inflation variability, and Japan has implemented wide-ranging financial-market deregulation in recent years. Furthermore, the competitiveness of the German financial system remains restricted in several ways. There is no market for short-term commercial paper; the equity market is extremely narrow; and futures trading has lagged behind developments in other major financial centers. Finally, although the proportion of Germany's exports consisting of differentiated manufactured products has risen, increases were also registered by the United States and Japan.

4 Recent Trends

To understand how the various determining factors have combined to influence the actual internationalization of the deutsche mark, we should examine data on the use of the mark as a medium of exchange, unit of account, and store of value.

Currency-Invoicing Patterns

The currency-invoicing patterns of German exports and imports from 1980 to 1988 are shown in Table 7. There has been little change in the currency denomination of Germany's exports, approximately 82 percent of which remain invoiced in deutsche marks. There has been a nearly 10-percent rise, however, in the share of German imports denominated in deutsche marks over the same period; this increase has been mainly at the expense of imports denominated in U.S. dollars.

Several points are worth making in this regard. First, the declining proportion of German imports from developing countries implies a corresponding increase in the share of imports denominated in deutsche marks, to the extent that developing-country exports (i.e., mainly primary products) are denominated in U.S. dollars. The decline in imports invoiced in U.S. dollars is at least partly explainable by this fact. Second, the redirection of German trade has raised the proportion of trade with European countries; about 70 percent of German imports were from EC countries in 1988, compared with 62 percent in 1980.[9] Because EC countries have invoiced a growing proportion of their exports in deutsche

[9] Data Resources (1990).

TABLE 7

CURRENCY INVOICING OF GERMAN FOREIGN TRADE
(percent of total exports or imports)

Currency	1980	1981	1982	1983	1984	1985	1986	1987	1988
				Exports					
Deutsche mark	82.5	82.2	83.2	82.6	79.4	79.5	81.5	81.5	n.a.
U.S. dollar	7.2	7.8	6.7	7.0	9.7	9.5	7.7	7.4	n.a.
Pound sterling	1.4	1.3	1.3	1.5	1.7	1.8	1.7	1.8	n.a.
Yen	0.0	0.0	0.0	0.0	0.3	0.4	0.4	0.5	n.a.
French franc	2.8	2.8	2.8	2.8	2.8	2.7	2.7	2.5	n.a.
Swiss franc	0.5	0.5	0.5	0.5	0.5	0.5	0.5	0.6	n.a.
Other	5.6	5.6	5.5	5.8	5.7	5.7	5.5	5.7	n.a.
				Imports					
Deutsche mark	43.0	43.0	44.6	46.1	47.0	47.8	51.7	52.7	52.6
U.S. dollar	32.3	32.3	31.3	28.8	29.2	28.1	23.1	22.0	21.6
Pound sterling	3.4	3.7	2.5	2.7	2.4	3.0	2.3	2.5	2.4
Yen	0.0	0.0	0.0	0.0	0.0	1.8	2.6	2.5	2.5
French franc	3.3	3.0	3.4	3.5	3.6	3.8	4.1	3.9	3.6
Swiss franc	1.6	1.6	1.6	1.5	1.5	1.5	1.7	1.8	1.7
Other [a]	15.4	16.4	16.6	17.4	16.5	14.0	14.5	14.9	15.6

SOURCE: Deutsche Bundesbank, unpublished data.

NOTE: Numbers are rounded and may not add up to 100.

[a] Includes trade invoiced in ECUs, the share of which was less than 0.1 percent of total imports in each year.

marks, this also helps explain the increase in the deutsche-mark denomination of German imports and illustrates a regional process underlying the increased use of the mark.[10] Increased use of the deutsche mark has been due in good measure to its key-currency role within Europe, and recent actions taken to broaden trade and financial connections between Western and Eastern Europe should contribute further to its wider use. At the start of 1990, for example, the Yugoslav dinar was pegged to the deutsche mark.

World-invoicing patterns are shown in Table 8, which uses data provided by Page (1981) and Black (1989) on the currency compositions of exports and imports for the six largest industrial countries and for OPEC. Page and Black provide data on the proportion of each country's exports

[10] In 1980, 9 percent of French exports were denominated in deutsche marks; in 1987, the figure was 10 percent. For Italy, the share of exports denominated in deutsche marks rose from 14 percent in 1980 to 18 percent in 1987 (Black, 1989).

TABLE 8

CURRENCY DENOMINATIONS OF WORLD EXPORTS
(*percent of world exports*)

Exporter	DM		US.$		£ Stg		¥		Fr. F		Lit	
	1980	1987	1980	1987	1980	1987	1980	1987	1980	1987	1980	1987
Germany	8.4	10.2	0.7	0.9	0.2	0.2	0.0	0.1	0.3	0.3	0.0	0.2
Unites States [a]	0.1	0.2	11.3	10.2	0.1	0.1	0.0	0.1	0.1	0.1	0.0	0.1
United Kingdom	0.2	0.2	1.0	0.9	4.4	4.3	0.0	0.0	0.1	0.1	0.0	0.0
Japan	0.1	0.2	4.5	6.2	0.1	0.1	2.0	3.3	0.0	0.1	0.0	0.0
France	0.6	0.6	0.8	0.7	0.2	0.2	0.0	0.0	3.5	3.9	0.0	0.3
Italy	0.6	0.9	1.2	1.0	0.3	0.0	0.0	0.0	0.0	0.4	1.5	1.9
OPEC [a]	0.2	0.1	15.0	4.9	0.2	0.1	0.0	0.0	0.2	0.1	0.2	0.1
Total	10.2	12.4	34.5	24.8	5.5	5.0	2.0	3.5	4.1	5.0	1.7	2.6

SOURCES: International Monetary Fund, *Direction of Trade Statistics Yearbook 1989*; Ministries of Finance of Germany, France, Italy, and Japan; Page, 1981; Black, 1989.

[a] 1987 figures based on estimates of currency denomination made by Black, 1989.

and imports invoiced in a certain currency; Table 8 adjusts these proportions for each country's share of world trade. In the case of Germany, for example, 82 percent of German exports were denominated in deutsche marks in 1980, and the German share of world exports was 12.5 percent. The product of these two numbers (10.2 percent) was Germany's contribution to the share of world exports denominated in deutsche marks. Calculating this share for other countries reveals that at least 34.5 percent of world exports were denominated in U.S. dollars in 1980 (the six largest industrial countries and OPEC jointly accounted for 60.5 percent of world exports in 1980 and 55.2 percent in 1987). In 1987, by contrast, 24.8 percent of world exports were denominated in U.S. dollars, and 12.4 percent were denominated in deutsche marks. Thus, the share of world exports denominated in U.S. dollars fell by 9.7 percentage points over the period, whereas the shares denominated in deutsche marks and yen rose by 2.2 and 1.5 percentage points, respectively. This calculation assumes, of course, that the export-invoicing behavior of other countries remained unchanged.

The Deutsche Mark as a Medium of Exchange

Trends in the volume of currencies traded on foreign-exchange markets can be used as proxies for trends in the relative importance of currencies as units of account and as mediums of exchange. Data on turnover in the interbank markets are available from surveys conducted by central banks in New York, London, and Tokyo in March 1986, April 1989, and at earlier dates in New York. These data, summarized in Table 9, show that the U.S. dollar continues to dominate the interbank market, that the share of the deutsche mark has been rather stable, and that the share of the yen has grown.

TABLE 9

CURRENCY COMPOSITION OF TURNOVER IN MAJOR FOREIGN-EXCHANGE MARKETS
(*percent of total turnover*)

Currency	New York				London		Tokyo	
	March 1980	April 1983	March 1986	April 1989	March 1986	April 1989	March 1986	April 1989
Against U.S. dollar								
Deutsche mark	31.8	32.5	34.2	32.9	28.0	22.0	10.4	9.7
Pound sterling	22.7	16.6	18.6	14.6	30.0	27.0	3.0	4.3
Yen	10.2	22.0	23.0	25.2	14.0	15.0	77.0	72.1
French franc	6.9	4.4	3.6	3.2	4.0	4.0	0.3	0.2
Swiss franc	10.1	12.2	9.7	11.8	9.0	10.0	5.6	4.4
Canadian dollar	12.2	7.5	5.2	4.0	2.0	2.0	0.0	0.0
Other	6.1	4.6	5.8	8.3	10.0	11.0	3.3	3.2
Cross-currency	n.a.	0.2	n.a.	n.a.	3.0	9.0	0.0	6.1

SOURCES: Federal Reserve Bank of New York, Bank of England, Bank of Japan, press releases, September 13, 1989.

NOTE: Numbers are rounded and may not add up to 100.

Another measure of a currency's role as an international medium of exchange is its use as an intervention vehicle by central banks. Table 10 gives data on this use of the deutsche mark within the EMS from 1979 through 1989, reporting both obligatory and discretionary (intramarginal) interventions. The figures show that there has been a substantial increase in the use of the deutsche mark in intervention.

Although these data show an increase in the absolute amount of deutsche-mark intervention, they do not trace changes in its share of the total. Table 11 reports the currency distribution of EMS intervention for three periods from March 1979 to June 1987. The data are based on those in Mastropasqua et al. (1988), who report the currency distributions of intervention in the EMS in U.S. dollars, EMS currencies, and other currencies but do not break out intervention in deutsche marks. The numbers show that the share of U.S.-dollar intervention fell from 71.5

TABLE 10

INTERVENTION IN THE EMS IN DEUTSCHE MARKS
(purchases and sales in billions of DM)

Year	Obligatory	Intramarginal	Total
1979 [a]	3.6	10.8	14.4
1980	5.9	6.9	12.8
1981	19.6	20.9	40.5
1982	3.0	22.2	25.2
1983	25.0	32.0	57.0
1984	4.7	37.8	42.5
1985	0.4	60.4	60.7
1986	23.1	109.6	132.7
1987	15.0	109.5	124.5
1988	0.0	43.1	43.1
1989	10.0	29.0	39.0

SOURCE: Deutsche Bundesbank, *Report of the Deutsche Bundesbank*, various issues, 1980-90.

[a] From March 1979.

percent in 1979-82 to 26.3 percent in 1986-87.[11] When data on deutsche-mark intervention are compiled for these periods, using the Bundesbank's *Reports* (1980-90), it is clear that the decline in the share of dollar intervention was largely the counterpart of an increase in the share of deutsche-mark intervention.[12]

Finally, Table 11 reports the currency distribution of intervention by the U.S. Federal Reserve and Treasury over approximately the same periods. This intervention has been entirely in terms of deutsche marks or yen. Although the data show a decline in the deutsche mark's share, it nevertheless accounted for more than half of U.S. intervention in 1986-88.

The Deutsche Mark as an Investment Currency

For purposes of exposition, foreign deutsche-mark claims can be classified into three broad categories: (1) claims held in Germany by foreigners,

[11] Some of this decline could be due to the valuation effects of exchange-rate changes. Nevertheless, these data are indicative of longer-term trends. This observation also applies to the data on investment uses of currencies, presented below.

[12] The Bundesbank figures are available only in terms of deutsche marks, whereas Mastropasqua et al. report their figures in U.S. dollars. The Bundesbank figures have therefore been converted into dollars using the average deutsche-mark-to-dollar exchange rate for each period.

TABLE 11

CURRENCY DISTRIBUTION OF FOREIGN-EXCHANGE INTERVENTION
(percent of total intervention)

Currency	Intervention in the EMS		
	1979-82 [a]	1983-85	1986-87 [b]
U.S. dollars	71.5	53.7	26.3
EMS currencies	27.2	43.5	71.7
[Deutsche marks]	[23.7]	[39.4]	[59.0]
Others [c]	1.3	2.8	2.0
	U.S. Federal Reserve and Treasury Intervention		
	1979-82	1983-85	1986-88
Deutsche marks	89.7	67.9	57.5
Yen	10.3	32.1	42.5

SOURCES: Deutsche Bundesbank, *Report of the Deutsche Bundesbank*, various issues, 1980-90; *Federal Reserve Bank of New York, Quarterly Review*, various issues, 1980-89; Mastropasqua et al., 1988.

NOTE: Total intervention includes both purchases and sales.

[a] From March 1979.

[b] To June 1987.

[c] From 1985, includes intervention in private ECUs.

which can be claims on German banks, enterprises, or the public sector, and can be short or long term; (2) claims held outside Germany by foreigners in the form of Euro-DM (short-term) deposits, typically with foreign offices or subsidiaries of German banks; and (3) claims held outside Germany by foreigners in the form of Euro-DM (long-term) bonds.[13]

Data pertaining to these categories are presented in Table 12. Deutsche-mark claims in Germany held by foreigners, which accounted for about 60 percent of foreigners' total claims in Germany at the end of 1987, more than doubled between 1980 and 1986 (Fröhlich, 1988). Approximately half of the increase took place in 1985 and 1986. This large increase has been attributed in part to the measures taken to deregulate the financial system at the end of 1984 and in 1985 (Reinhold

[13] This is the categorization of the Bundesbank, which uses a narrow definition of deutsche-mark claims held outside Germany and excludes claims outside Germany held by German residents. This definition differs from that used by the Bank for International Settlements (see below).

and Oldenbourg, 1986; Deutsche Bundesbank, 1987; and Thomas, 1987). The abolition of the coupon tax on interest payments to foreigners and the introduction of more flexible financial instruments make it more attractive for foreigners to invest in the German financial system. Foreigners' net purchases of domestic bonds rose from DM 13.8 billion in 1984 to DM 59.1 billion in 1986 (see memorandum item in Table 12).

TABLE 12

FOREIGN DEUTSCHE-MARK CLAIMS

(billions of DM and percent of category)

Type of Claim	1980 [a]	1982	1984	1986	1988	1989
Held in Germany on:						
German banking system	106.0	121.0	143.0	178.0	195.0	222.0
Enterprises and individuals [b]	69.0	86.0	107.0	164.0	149.0	165.0
Public sector [c]	31.0	85.0	109.0	166.0	192.0	198.0
Total [d]	206.0	292.0	359.0	508.0	536.0	585.0
Percent long-term	61.8	60.3	64.2	75.7	75.0	72.0
Percent short-term	38.2	39.7	35.8	24.3	25.0	28.0
Held outside Germany [e]	266.0	303.0	376.0	383.0	516.0	599.0
Euro-DM as percent of all Eurodollars, Euroyen, and Euro-DM deposits [f]	n.a.	12.3	10.8	12.3	13.7	14.2
Held as external deutsche-mark bonds [g]	57.0	61.0	71.0	102.0	124.0	128.0
Memorandum item:						
Net purchases or sales of domestic bonds by foreigners	0.3	2.3	13.8	59.1	2.1	0.7

SOURCES: Deutsche Bundesbank *Report of the Deutsche Bundesbank*, various issues, 1980-90; Fröhlich, 1988.

[a] Mid-year data for 1980, 1982, and 1989; end-of-year data for 1984, 1986, and 1988.

[b] Includes bond issues of the Federal Railways and Federal Post Office.

[c] Includes deutsche-mark notes held by foreigners (estimated).

[d] Includes direct investments, other equity holdings, and real estate transactions, and also foreign claims in instruments denominated in other currencies.

[e] Banks in the European reporting area and in Canada and Japan.

[f] Dollar liabilities in the European reporting area (here including Germany), Japan, and Canada, as well as liabilities of international banking facilities and of certain offshore branches of U.S. banks to depositors outside the United States; yen liabilities of banks in the European reporting area to depositors outside Japan; and deutsche-mark liabilities of banks outside Germany to non-German depositors.

[g] Computed from data on the total outstanding (face value) and estimated domestic holdings.

External deutsche-mark claims held by foreigners also rose between 1980 and 1986 but at a slower rate than claims held in Germany. In 1980, total external claims (Euromarket claims and external deutsche-mark bonds) were about one and one-half times foreign claims held in Germany; by 1986, foreign claims held in Germany had surpassed external claims. This development is also explained in part by the liberalization measures introduced in 1984 and 1985; there was a substitution of deutsche-mark investments in Germany for the holding of external deutsche-mark claims.

Announcement of the withholding tax in the fourth quarter of 1987 worked to reverse this substitution. External deutsche-mark claims held by foreigners rose by 17 percent in 1987, whereas foreign claims held in Germany declined.[14] Similarly, foreigners' net purchases of domestic bonds fell from DM 59.1 billion in 1986 to DM 35.0 billion in 1987. Lipschitz et al. (1989, p. 48) have noted that the major part of the proposed withholding tax was reflected in the relative yields of foreign and domestic deutsche-mark bonds. The tax decreased the demand for domestic instruments, thereby lowering their prices and raising their yields. The average yield on German public-authority bonds was more than 50 basis points lower than the average yield on issues by foreign public bodies in the first nine months of 1987; this differential disappeared almost entirely following the announcement of the withholding tax, and, by August 1988, foreign issues were trading at yields about 25 points lower than German issues. Similarly, net purchases of domestic bonds by foreigners fell from DM 59.1 billion in 1986 to DM 35.0 billion in 1987.

Announcement of the abolition of the withholding tax in April 1989 contributed to a sharp increase in foreign deutsche-mark claims held in Germany during the first half of 1989, but external deutsche-mark claims also rose. In the period from 1980 through the first half of 1989, foreigners' deutsche-mark claims in Germany increased by over 180 percent, and those held externally rose by 125 percent.

Table 12 also shows that foreigners' deutsche-mark claims in Germany have been predominantly long term, and that the share of long-term claims rose during the 1980s. This reflects, in part, Germany's comparative disadvantage in providing short-term financial instruments, a position that in turn restricts the efficiency of the German financial market in

[14] Although the announcement of the withholding tax did not occur until the fourth quarter, it had a marked impact on foreign claims held in Germany. They rose from DM 508 billion in December 1986 to DM 539 billion in June 1987 but fell to DM 497 billion in December 1987.

international liquidity transformation.

To assess the relative performance of the deutsche mark in international capital markets, Table 13 presents data on the use of various currencies as stores of value and units of account from 1981 through

TABLE 13

RELATIVE CURRENCY SHARES OF EXTERNAL ASSETS

(percent)

Asset Type and Currency	1981-84(Avg)[a]	1985	1986	1987	1988	1989[b]
Shares of external bank loans[c]						
Deutsche mark	1.7	2.1	3.0	2.4	2.2	3.2
U.S. dollar	83.3	62.5	67.0	65.1	69.9	77.0
Pound sterling	3.1	3.4	6.4	14.7	14.1	6.4
Yen	5.9	18.5	16.1	10.8	5.6	5.3
Swiss franc	1.2	3.0	2.1	0.7	0.3	0.4
ECU	1.3	7.1	2.2	2.4	2.8	4.6
Other	3.5	3.4	3.2	3.9	5.1	3.1
Denominations of external bond issues[d]						
Deutsche mark	6.3	8.5	8.0	8.0	10.1	6.4
U.S. dollar	63.2	54.0	53.9	38.8	41.2	51.9
Pound sterling	3.4	4.0	4.6	7.8	9.4	6.8
Yen	5.7	9.1	10.4	13.7	8.4	8.3
Swiss franc	14.7	11.3	10.7	12.9	11.1	7.5
ECU	1.7	5.2	3.4	4.0	4.9	5.2
Other	6.7	7.9	9.0	14.8	14.9	13.9
Denominations of Eurocurrency deposits						
Deutsche mark	11.4	11.4	12.8	14.2	13.3	13.9
U.S. dollar	74.0	67.9	63.5	58.2	60.1	59.7
Pound sterling	1.4	2.0	2.1	2.8	3.4	3.1
Yen	1.8	3.4	4.5	5.8	5.5	5.5
Swiss franc	5.8	6.4	7.2	7.7	5.4	4.9
ECU	0.5[e]	2.6	2.6	2.8	3.0	3.2
Other[f]	5.2	6.2	7.2	8.4	9.2	9.7

SOURCES: Organisation for Economic Co-operation and Development, *Financial Market Trends*, Nos. 30-46, 1985-90; Bank for International Settlements, *Annual Report* and *International Banking and Financial Market Developments*, various issues, 1980-90.

NOTE: Numbers are rounded and may not add up to 100.

[a] 1980 data not comparable to subsequent years, so average taken from 1981-84.

[b] Data for Eurocurrency deposits are through September 1989.

[c] Foreign and international bank loans, excluding loans renegotiated.

[d] Includes international issues, foreign issues, and special placements.

[e] Included in "other" category prior to 1983.

[f] Includes foreign-currency position of banks in the United States, for which no currency breakdown is available.

1989. Currency use is classified as external bank loans, which include foreign and international bank loans; external bond issues, which include foreign and international issues and special placements; and Eurocurrency deposits. These data were compiled by the Bank for International Settlements (BIS) and differ in coverage from the data in Table 12 in that they include resident holdings in external bond issues and Eurocurrency deposits. In general, they indicate a growing role for the deutsche mark in international capital markets.

The importance of currencies as stores of value can also be gauged from their use as reserve assets. Table 14 presents currency shares in official holdings of foreign exchange by all reporting countries and by selected EC countries from 1980 through 1989. The data for all countries show that the largest gain was registered by the deutsche mark (4.7 percentage points); its share reached nearly 20 percent in 1989. The data

TABLE 14

CURRENCY SHARES OF OFFICIAL FOREIGN-EXCHANGE HOLDINGS, 1980-89

(percent)

Currency	1980	1982	1984	1986	1988	1989 [a]
		All Countries				
Deutsche mark	14.9	11.7	11.6	13.7	16.0	19.6
U.S. dollar	68.6	70.4	69.3	66.0	63.8	59.2
Pound sterling	2.9	2.3	2.9	2.6	2.8	2.8
Yen	4.3	4.6	5.5	7.5	7.7	8.1
French franc	1.7	1.1	0.8	0.9	1.2	1.2
Swiss franc	3.2	2.4	2.0	1.9	2.0	2.0
Netherlands guilder	1.3	1.1	0.7	1.0	1.1	1.0
Unspecified currencies	3.1	6.1	7.0	6.4	5.4	6.0
		Selected EC Countries [b]				
Deutsche mark	12.0	10.3	16.6	14.9	20.3	23.4
U.S. dollar	80.2	80.9	72.9	71.3	63.7	57.9
Pound sterling	1.0	0.8	1.4	1.7	1.3	0.7
Yen	2.0	3.5	4.7	6.2	6.7	4.7
French franc	0.8	0.2	0.1	0.1	1.4	1.4
Swiss franc	1.0	1.6	1.8	2.1	2.2	2.1
Netherlands guilder	1.0	1.0	0.8	1.1	1.0	1.2
Unspecified currencies	1.9	1.8	1.8	2.8	3.4	8.7

SOURCES: International Monetary Fund, *Annual Report*, various issues, 1978-90, and IMF staff estimates.

NOTE: Numbers are rounded and may not add up to 100.

[a] End-of-year data.

[b] Data are IMF staff estimates and are in some instances based on interpolations.

for EC countries show a more striking rise in the share of the deutsche mark (11.4 percentage points); this rise was at the expense of U.S. dollar.

5 Conclusions

This paper has examined conditions affecting the international use of a currency, reviewed recent developments affecting use of the deutsche mark, and presented data on the internationalization of the deutsche mark during the 1980s.

Theoretical considerations indicate that several factors combine to advance the internationalization of a currency: (1) a relatively low rate of inflation and low inflation variability (predominantly the result of credible government policies) and a relatively stable external value; (2) open, deep, and broad financial markets; and (3) the share a country has of world exports and the composition of its trade, that is, the share of differentiated manufactured goods in its exports and, to a lesser extent, the share of developing countries in its trade. Recent developments presage an expanding role for the deutsche mark, and the data corroborate this expectation. They show that the world has been moving to a multicurrency monetary system and that the deutsche mark is emerging as a key currency in that system. They also show that the expanding international role of the deutsche mark has stemmed in substantial measure from its importance as a key currency in Europe. The increase in deutsche-mark invoicing by European countries has more than offset any lessening of invoicing in deutsche marks that must have resulted from the declining share of Germany's trade with developing countries. Furthermore, there has been a striking increase in the use of the deutsche mark for intervention within the EMS. Indeed, German monetary policy has led to the use of the deutsche mark as the effective currency peg in the EMS. There has also been an increase in European use of the deutsche mark as a reserve asset.

Given the deutsche mark's role as the key currency in Europe, the economic and monetary integration of both Germany and Europe is likely to enhance its position as an international currency. German unification should contribute to wider use of the deutsche mark, provided it does not undermine its internal value.[15] European integration may, however,

[15] Remarks by Bundesbank president Karl Otto Pöhl in March 1991 calling unification a "disaster" are indicative of a bumpy road ahead. Mr. Pöhl's comments reflected concerns following the Bundesbank's announcement that pan-German money supply (M-3) was 19.5 percent higher in January 1991 than M-3 had been in the former West Germany in January 1990.

culminate in the creation of a European central bank and the use of a new, single, European currency, the European Currency Unit (ECU). The introduction of the ECU would have several advantages over a system of national monies linked by fixed exchange rates, including the elimination of transaction costs and exchange-rate risk and the attainment of complete financial-market integration. If European union does proceed in that direction, it seems reasonable to infer that the reputation of the deutsche mark will give credibility to the new currency.

APPENDIX

MEASURES FOR CONTROLLING CAPITAL INFLOWS INTO GERMANY, 1970-89

Date	Measure
May 1971	Reintroduction, at the beginning of the "dollar crisis," of the authorization requirement for nonresident purchases of domestic money-market paper and for the payment of interest on foreign deposits with domestic banks.
March 1972	Introduction of the cash-deposit requirement for borrowings abroad. Exceptions for credits in connection with the use of customary terms of payment and in relation to specific goods and services supplied. Cash-deposit ratio initially at 40 percent, with an exemption limit of DM 2 million.
June 1972	Introduction of the authorization requirement for nonresident purchases of domestic bonds from residents.
July 1972	Raising of the cash-deposit ratio to 50 percent and reduction of the cash-deposit exemption limit to DM 500,000.
January 1973	Reduction of the cash-deposit exemption limit to DM 50,000.
February 1973	Extension of the authorization requirement to nonresident purchases of equities. Introduction of the authorization requirement for residents borrowing abroad.
June 1973	Introduction of the authorization requirement for the assignment of domestic claims to nonresidents.
February 1974	Reduction of the cash-deposit ratio to 20 percent and raising of the cash-deposit exemption limit to DM 100,000. Restriction of the authorization requirement regarding nonresident purchases of domestic securities to bonds with (remaining) maturities of up to four years. Removal of the authorization requirement for residents borrowing abroad.
September 1974	Removal of the cash-deposit requirement and the authorization requirement for the assignment of domestic claims to nonresidents.
September 1975	Removal of the authorization requirement for the payment of interest on foreign deposits with domestic banks and further relaxation of the authorization requirement for nonresident purchases of domestic bonds.
March 1980	Assignment allowed of official borrowers' notes to nonresidents. Authorizations for nonresident purchases of domestic bonds with (remaining) maturities of more than two years normally granted.

November 1980	Authorizations for nonresident purchases of domestic bonds with (remaining) maturities of more than one year normally granted.
March 1981	Nonresident purchases of any domestic bonds and money-market paper normally approved.
August 1981	Removal of all remaining authorization restrictions on nonresident purchases of domestic bonds and money-market paper.
December 1984	Introduction of act, retroactive to August 1984, governing the abolition of coupon tax on interest received by nonresidents from domestic bonds.
May 1985	Permission, effective from May 1, for resident foreign-owned banks to lead-manage issues of foreign DM bonds, subject to granting of similar privileges to German-owned banks resident in the home countries of the foreign banks in question.
May 1985	Introduction of zero-coupon bonds, floating-rate notes, and swap-related bonds in the capital market permitted by the Bundesbank.
May 1986	Admission of foreign banks to an enlarged Federal Bond Consortium (with government, helps supervise new bond issues). Required reserves of most foreign-currency liabilities to nonresidents abolished.
July 1989	Across-the-board reduction of minimum maturities to two years for public offerings and public placements allowed by the Bundesbank.

SOURCE: Deutsche Bundesbank, *Monthly Report*, various issues.

References

Aschheim, Joseph, and Y. S. Park, *Artificial Currency Units: The Formation of Functional Currency Areas*, Essays in International Finance No. 114, Princeton, N.J., Princeton University, International Finance Section, April 1976.

Bailey, Martin J., and George S. Tavlas, "Trade and Investment Performance Under Floating Exchange Rates: The U.S. Experience," *Cato Journal*, 8 (Fall 1988), pp. 421-442.

———, "Exchange Rate Variability and Direct Investment," *Annals of the American Academy of Political and Social Science*, forthcoming (1991).

Bank for International Settlements *Annual Report*, various issues, Basle, Bank for International Settlements, 1980-1990.

———, *International Banking and Financial Market Developments*, various issues, Basle, Bank for International Settlements, 1980-1990.

Bilson, John, "The Choice of an Invoice Currency in International Transaction," in Jagdeep S. Bhandari and Bluford H. Putnam, eds., *Economic Interdependence and Flexible Exchange Rates*, Cambridge, Mass., MIT Press, 1983, pp. 384-401.

———, "The ECU and the Choice of an Invoice Currency," in Richard M. Levich and Andrea Sommariva, eds., *The ECU Market*, Lexington, Mass., Lexington Books, 1987, pp. 145-155.

Black, Stanley, "Transactions Costs and Vehicle Currencies," International Monetary Fund Working Paper 89/96, Washington, D.C., International Monetary Fund, November 1989.

Carse, Stephen, John Williamson, and Geoffrey E. Woods, *The Financing Procedures of British Foreign Trade*, Cambridge, Cambridge University Press, 1980.

Chrystal, Alec, "On the Theory of International Money," in John Black and Graeme S. Dorrance, eds., *Problems of International Finance,* New York, St. Martin's Press, 1984, pp. 77-92.

Cohen, Benjamin, *The Future of Sterling as an International Currency*, London, Macmillan, 1971.

Data Resources, *World Trade Model Data Bank*, Lexington, Mass., Data Resources, 1990.

Deutsche Bundesbank, "External Assets and Liabilities of the Federal Republic of Germany," *Monthly Report*, 31 (October 1979), pp. 27-34.

———, "The Deutsche Mark as an International Investment Currency," *Monthly Report*, 36 (January 1984), pp. 13-20.

———, "Freedom of Germany's Capital Transaction with Foreign Countries," *Monthly Report*, 37 (July 1985), pp. 13-23.

———, "Foreign Deutsche Mark Assets and Liabilities," *Monthly Report*, 39 (May 1987), pp. 34-42.

———, "Forty Years of the Deutsche Mark," *Monthly Report*, 40 (May 1988), pp. 13-23.

———, *Report of the Deutsche Bundesbank*, various issues, Frankfurt, Johannes

Weisbecker, 1980-1990.
Dornbusch, Rudiger, "Flexible Exchange Rates and Excess Capital Mobility," *Brookings Papers on Economic Activity*, No. 1, 1986, pp. 209-226.
Federal Reserve Bank of New York, "Summary of Results of U.S. Foreign Exchange Market Survey Conducted in April 1989," Press Release, September 13, 1989.
Federal Reserve Bank of New York Quarterly Review, 5 through 14 (Spring 1980 through Fall 1989).
Financial Times (London), "Britain and the EMS," September 28, 1987.
Fischer, Stanley, "British Monetary Policy," in Rudiger Dornbusch and Richard Layard, eds., *The Performance of the British Economy*, Oxford, Oxford University Press, 1987, pp. 6-28.
Frankel, Jeffrey, "The World's Key Currencies," paper presented at the Fourth Nikkei Teleconference, April 1989.
Fratianni, Michael, "The Dollar and the ECU," in Jacob S. Dreyer, Gottfried Haberler, and Thomas Willett, eds., *The International Monetary System*, Washington, D.C., American Enterprise Institute, 1982, pp. 430-453.
Frenkel, Jacob, and Morris Goldstein, "A Guide to Target Zones," *International Monetary Fund Staff Papers*, 33 (December 1986), pp. 663-673.
Fröhlich, Hans Peter, "Weltwährung D-Mark," Beiträge zur Wirtschafts- und Sozialpolitik, Cologne, Institut der deutschen Wirtschaft, processed, September 1988.
Giavazzi, Francesco, and Alberto Giovannini, *Limited Exchange Rate Flexibility*, Cambridge, Mass., MIT Press, 1989.
Glynn, Lenny, "The Greenback is Back," *Institutional Investor*, September 1989, pp. 157-163.
Goldstein, Morris, *The Exchange Rate System: Lessons of the Past and Options for the Future*, Occasional Paper 30, Washington, D.C., International Monetary Fund, July 1984.
Grassman, Sven, "A Fundamental Symmetry in International Payments Patterns," *Journal of International Economics*, 3 (May 1973), pp. 105-116.
International Monetary Fund, *Annual Report*, various issues, Washington, D.C., International Monetary Fund, 1978-1990.
———, *Direction of Trade Statistics Yearbook 1989*, Washington, D.C., International Monetary Fund, 1989.
———, *International Financial Statistics*, various issues, Washington, D.C., International Monetary Fund, 1981-1990.
Kenen, Peter B., *The Role of the Dollar as an International Currency*, Group of Thirty Occasional Paper 13, New York, Group of Thirty, 1983.
———, *Managing Exchange Rates*, Chatham House Papers, London and New York, The Royal Institute of International Affairs, 1988.
Klump, Rainer, "Der Dollar als internationale Schlüsselwährung," *Kredit und Kapital*, 3 (1989), pp. 375-402.
Krugman, Paul, "Vehicle Currencies and the Structure of International Exchange," *Journal of Money, Credit and Banking*, 12 (August 1980), pp. 513-526.

———, "The International Role of the Dollar: Theory and Prospect," in John Bilson and Richard S. Martson, eds., *Exchange Rate Theory and Practice*, Chicago, University of Chicago Press, 1984, pp. 261-278.

Levich, Richard M., "Development of the ECU Market: Perspective on Financial Innovation," in Richard M. Levich and Andrea Sommariva, eds., *The ECU Market*, Lexington, Mass., Lexington Books, 1987, pp. 103-116.

Lipschitz, Leslie, Jeroen Kremers, Thomas Mayer, and Donogh McDonald, *The Federal Republic of Germany: Adjustment in a Surplus Country*, Occasional Paper 64, Washington, D.C., International Monetary Fund, January 1989.

McKinnon, Ronald I., *Money in International Exchange*, New York, Oxford University Press, 1979.

Magee, Stephen, and Ramesh Rao, "Vehicle and Nonvehicle Currencies in International Trade," *American Economic Review*, 70 (May 1980), pp. 368-373.

Mastropasqua, Christina, Stefano Micossi, and Roberto Rinaldi, "Interventions, Sterilization and Monetary Policy in European Monetary System Countries, 1979-87," in Francesco Giavazzi, Stefano Micossi, and Marcus Miller, eds., *The European Monetary System*, Cambridge, Cambridge University Press, 1988, pp. 252-291.

Melitz, Jacques, "Monetary Discipline and Cooperation in the European Monetary System: A Synthesis," in Francesco Giavazzi, Stefano Micossi, and Marcus Miller, eds., *The European Monetary System*, Cambridge, Cambridge University Press, 1988, pp. 51-79.

Neumann, Manfred J., "Internationalization of German Banking and Finance" in Korea Federation of Banks, *Internationalization of Banking: Analysis and Prospects*, Seoul, Korea Federation of Banks, 1986, pp. 67-144.

Organisation for Economic Co-operation and Development, *Financial Market Trends*, Nos. 30-46, Paris, Organisation for Economic Co-operation and Development, 1985-1990.

Page, S.A.B., "Currency of Invoicing in Merchandise Trade," *National Institute Economic Review*, 81 (August 1977), pp. 77-81.

———, "The Choices of Invoicing Currency in Merchandise Trade," *National Institute Economic Review*, 85 (November 1981), pp. 60-72.

Reinhold, Rolf, and Thomas Oldenbourg, "Auslandsbanken im Liberalisierten DM--Kapitalmarket," *Deutsche Bundesbank, Auszüge aus Presseartikeln*, No. 74, November 3, 1986, pp. 4-6.

Rieke, Wolfgang, "The Development of the Deutsche Mark as a Reserve Currency," in Group of Thirty, *Reserve Currencies in Transition*, New York, Group of Thirty, 1982, pp. 16-23.

Scharrer, Hans-Eckart, "Currencies and Currency Hedging in German Foreign Trade," in Deutsche Bank, *Studies on Economic and Monetary Problems and on Banking History*, No. 18, Bonn, 1980, pp. 3-25.

Storch, Gunter, "Germany as a Financial Centre," *Deutsche Bundesbank, Auszüge aus Presseartikeln*, No. 54 , July 3, 1989, pp.7-9.

Swamy, P.A.V.B., and George S. Tavlas, "Financial Deregulation, the Demand for Money, and Monetary Policy in Australia," *International Monetary Fund Staff*

Papers, 36 (March 1989), pp. 69-101.
———, "Is It Possible to Find an Econometric Law that Works Well in Explanation and Prediction? The Case of Australian Money Demand," *Journal of Forecasting*, 10, forthcoming (1991).
Tavlas, George S., and Yusuro Ozeki, "The Japanese Yen as an International Currency," International Monetary Fund Working Paper 91/2, Washington, D.C., International Monetary Fund, January 1991.
Thomas, Karl, "DM-Auslandsanleihen und Innovationen am deutschen Kapitalmarket," *Deutsche Bundesbank, Auszüge aus Presseartikeln*, No. 21 (March 20, 1987), pp. 5-7.
Ungerer, Horst, Owen Evans, Thomas Mayer, and Philip Young, *The European Monetary System: Recent Developments*, Occasional Paper 48, Washington, D.C., International Monetary Fund, December 1986.
Williams, David, "The Evolution of the Sterling System," in Charles R. Whittlesey and John S. G. Wilson, eds., *Essays in Money and Banking in Honour of R. S. Sayer*, Oxford, Oxford University Press, 1968, pp. 266-297.
Williamson, John, *The Exchange Rate System*, Washington, D.C., Institute for International Economics, June 1985.

PUBLICATIONS OF THE
INTERNATIONAL FINANCE SECTION

Notice to Contributors

The International Finance Section publishes papers in four series: ESSAYS IN INTERNATIONAL FINANCE, PRINCETON STUDIES IN INTERNATIONAL FINANCE, SPECIAL PAPERS IN INTERNATIONAL ECONOMICS, AND REPRINTS IN INTERNATIONAL FINANCE. ESSAYS, STUDIES, AND SPECIAL PAPERS contain new work not published elsewhere. REPRINTS reproduce journal articles previously published by Princeton faculty members associated with the Section. The Section welcomes the submission of manuscripts for publication under the following guidelines:

ESSAYS are meant to disseminate new views about international financial matters and should be accessible to well-informed nonspecialists as well as to professional economists. Technical terms, tables, and charts should be used sparingly; mathematics should be avoided.

STUDIES are devoted to new research on international finance, with preference given to empirical work. They should be comparable in originality and technical proficiency to papers published in leading economic journals. They should be of medium length, longer than a journal article but shorter than a book.

SPECIAL PAPERS are surveys of research on particular topics and should be suitable for use in undergraduate courses. They may be concerned with international trade as well as international finance. They should also be of medium length.

Manuscripts should be submitted in triplicate, typed single sided and double spaced throughout on 8½ by 11 white bond paper. Publication can be expedited if manuscripts are computer keyboarded in WordPerfect 5.1 or a compatible program. Additional instructions and a style guide are available from the Section.

How to Obtain Publications

The Section's publications are distributed free of charge to college, university, and public libraries and to nongovernmental, nonprofit research institutions. Eligible institutions may ask to be placed on the Section's permanent mailing list.

Individuals and institutions not qualifying for free distribution may receive all publications for the calendar year for a subscription fee of $30.00. Late subscribers will receive all back issues for the year during which they subscribe. Subscribers should notify the Section promptly of any change in address, giving the old address as well as the new.

Publications may be ordered individually, with payment made in advance. ESSAYS and REPRINTS cost $6.50 each; STUDIES and SPECIAL PAPERS cost $9.00. An additional $1.25 should be sent for postage and handling within the United States, Canada, and Mexico; $1.50 should be added for surface delivery outside the region.

All payments must be made in U.S. dollars. Subscription fees and charges for single issues will be waived for organizations and individuals in countries where foreign-exchange regulations prohibit dollar payments.

Please address all correspondence, submissions, and orders to:

International Finance Section
Department of Economics, Fisher Hall
Princeton University
Princeton, New Jersey 08544-1021

List of Recent Publications

A complete list of publications may be obtained from the International Finance Section.

ESSAYS IN INTERNATIONAL FINANCE

152. G. K. Helleiner, *The IMF and Africa in the 1980s*. (July 1983)
153. Rachel McCulloch, *Unexpected Real Consequences of Floating Exchange Rates*. (August 1983)
154. Robert M. Dunn, Jr., *The Many Disappointments of Flexible Exchange Rates*. (December 1983)
155. Stephen Marris, *Managing the World Economy: Will We Ever Learn?* (October 1984)
156. Sebastian Edwards, *The Order of Liberalization of the External Sector in Developing Countries*. (December 1984)
157. Wilfred J. Ethier and Richard C. Marston, eds., with Kindleberger, Guttentag and Herring, Wallich, Henderson, and Hinshaw, *International Financial Markets and Capital Movements: A Symposium in Honor of Arthur I. Bloomfield*. (September 1985)
158. Charles E. Dumas, *The Effects of Government Deficits: A Comparative Analysis of Crowding Out*. (October 1985)
159. Jeffrey A. Frankel, *Six Possible Meanings of "Overvaluation": The 1981-85 Dollar*. (December 1985)
160. Stanley W. Black, *Learning from Adversity: Policy Responses to Two Oil Shocks*. (December 1985)
161. Alexis Rieffel, *The Role of the Paris Club in Managing Debt Problems*. (December 1985)
162. Stephen E. Haynes, Michael M. Hutchison, and Raymond F. Mikesell, *Japanese Financial Policies and the U.S. Trade Deficit*. (April 1986)
163. Arminio Fraga, *German Reparations and Brazilian Debt: A Comparative Study*. (July 1986)
164. Jack M. Guttentag and Richard J. Herring, *Disaster Myopia in International Banking*. (September 1986)
165. Rudiger Dornbusch, *Inflation, Exchange Rates, and Stabilization*. (October 1986)
166. John Spraos, *IMF Conditionality: Ineffectual, Inefficient, Mistargeted*. (December 1986)

*Publications marked by an asterisk are out of print. They are available on demand in xerographic paperback or library-bound copies from University Microfilms International, Box 1467, Ann Arbor, Michigan 48106, USA, or 30-32 Mortimer St., London, WIN 7RA, England. Microfilm of all Essays by year is available from University Microfilms. Photocopied sheets of out-of-print titles are available from the Section at $9.00 per Essay and $11.00 per Study or Special Paper, plus $1.25 for domestic ($1.50 for overseas) postage and handling.

167. Rainer Stefano Masera, *An Increasing Role for the ECU: A Character in Search of a Script*. (June 1987)
168. Paul Mosley, *Conditionality as Bargaining Process: Structural-Adjustment Lending, 1980-86*. (October 1987)
169. Paul Volcker, Ralph Bryant, Leonhard Gleske, Gottfried Haberler, Alexandre Lamfalussy, Shijuro Ogata, Jesús Silva-Herzog, Ross Starr, James Tobin, and Robert Triffin, *International Monetary Cooperation: Essays in Honor of Henry C. Wallich*. (December 1987)
170. Shafiqul Islam, *The Dollar and the Policy-Performance-Confidence Mix*. (July 1988)
171. James M. Boughton, *The Monetary Approach to Exchange Rates: What Now Remains?* (October 1988)
172. Jack M. Guttentag and Richard M. Herring, *Accounting for Losses On Sovereign Debt: Implications for New Lending*. (May 1989)
173. Benjamin J. Cohen, *Developing-Country Debt: A Middle Way*. (May 1989)
174. Jeffrey D. Sachs, *New Approaches to the Latin American Debt Crisis*. (July 1989)
175. C. David Finch, *The IMF: The Record and the Prospect*. (September 1989)
176. Graham Bird, *Loan-loss Provisions and Third-World Debt*. (November 1989)
177. Ronald Findlay, *The "Triangular Trade" and the Atlantic Economy of the Eighteenth Century: A Simple General-Equilibrium Model*. (March 1990)
178. Alberto Giovannini, *The Transition to European Monetary Union*. (November 1990)
179. Michael L. Mussa, *Exchange Rates in Theory and in Reality*. (December 1990)
180. Warren L. Coats, Jr., Reinhard W. Furstenberg, and Peter Isard, *The SDR System and the Issue of Resource Transfers*. (December 1990)
181. George S. Tavlas, *On the International Use of Currencies: The Case of the Deutsche Mark*. (March 1991)

PRINCETON STUDIES IN INTERNATIONAL FINANCE

52. Irving B. Kravis and Robert E. Lipsey, *Toward an Explanation of National Price Levels*. (November 1983)
53. Avraham Ben-Basset, *Reserve-Currency Diversification and the Substitution Account*. (March 1984)
*54. Jeffrey Sachs, *Theoretical Issues in International Borrowing*. (July 1984)
55. Marsha R. Shelburn, *Rules for Regulating Intervention under a Managed Float*. (December 1984)
56. Paul De Grauwe, Marc Janssens and Hilde Leliaert, *Real-Exchange-Rate Variability from 1920 to 1926 and 1973 to 1982*. (September 1985)
57. Stephen S. Golub, *The Current-Account Balance and the Dollar: 1977-78 and 1983-84*. (October 1986)
58. John T. Cuddington, *Capital Flight: Estimates, Issues, and Explanations*. (December 1986)
59. Vincent P. Crawford, *International Lending, Long-Term Credit Relationships, and Dynamic Contract Theory*. (March 1987)

60. Thorvaldur Gylfason, *Credit Policy and Economic Activity in Developing Countries with IMF Stabilization Programs*. (August 1987)
61. Stephen A. Schuker, *American "Reparations" to Germany, 1919-33: Implications for the Third-World Debt Crisis*. (July 1988)
62. Steven B. Kamin, *Devaluation, External Balance, and Macroeconomic Performance: A Look at the Numbers*. (August 1988)
63. Jacob A. Frenkel and Assaf Razin, *Spending, Taxes, and Deficits: International-Intertemporal Approach*. (December 1988)
64. Jeffrey A. Frankel, *Obstacles to International Macroeconomic Policy Coordination*. (December 1988)
65. Peter Hooper and Catherine L. Mann, *The Emergence and Persistence of the U.S. External Imbalance, 1980-87*. (October 1989)
66. Helmut Reisen, *Public Debt, External Competitiveness, and Fiscal Discipline in Developing Countries*. (November 1989)
67. Victor Argy, Warwick McKibbin, and Eric Siegloff, *Exchange-Rate Regimes for a Small Economy in a Multi-Country World*. (December 1989)
68. Mark Gersovitz and Christina H. Paxson, *The Economies of Africa and the Prices of Their Exports*. (October 1990)
69. Felipe Larraín and Andrés Velasco, *Can Swaps Solve the Debt Crisis? Lessons from the Chilean Experience*. (November 1990)

SPECIAL PAPERS IN INTERNATIONAL ECONOMICS

15. Gene M. Grossman and J. David Richardson, *Strategic Trade Policy: A Survey of Issues and Early Analysis*. (April 1985)
16. Elhanan Helpman, *Monopolistic Competition in Trade Theory*. (June 1990)

REPRINTS IN INTERNATIONAL FINANCE

24. Peter B. Kenen, *Forward Rates, Interest Rates, and Expectations under Alternative Exchange Rate Regimes*; reprinted from *Economic Record* 61, 1985. (June 1986)
25. Jorge Braga de Macedo, *Trade and Financial Interdependence under Flexible Exchange Rates: The Pacific Area*; reprinted from *Pacific Growth and Financial Interdependence*, 1986. (June 1986)
26. Peter B. Kenen, *The Use of IMF Credit*; reprinted from *Pulling Together: The International Monetary Fund in a Multipolar World*, 1989. (December 1989)